LET'S LEARN ENGLISH

Second Language Activities for the Primary Grades

G. Yvonne Pérez
Idolina G. Vela
Carroll Frankenberger

Scott, Foresman and Company
Glenview, Illinois   London

 **Good Year Books**

are available for preschool through grade 12
and for every basic curriculum subject plus
many enrichment areas. For more Good Year
Books, contact your local bookseller or
educational dealer. For a complete catalog
with information about other Good Year
Books, please write:

Good Year Books
Department GYB
1900 East Lake Avenue
Glenview, Illinois 60025

ISBN 0-673-18371-8

CONTENTS

Preface

Let's Learn English is filled with motivating ideas and activities that can supplement any primary basal reading program or language development curriculum in kindergarten through third grade. Intended to be used by teachers of students who are learning English as a second language, it offers such students language learning experiences and creative opportunities to use newly acquired reading, speaking, and writing skills. In addition, it offers teachers an organized instructional plan for teaching English as a second language, thematic sets of functional and relevant vocabulary words, a variety of fun-filled activities, and a basic set of reading skills.

Let's Learn English is a resource rich in features that meet the special needs of the second language learner and his/her teacher. Students will discover lessons that are fun, motivating, relevant, and experientially based. Teachers will find an easily identifiable instructional plan, clear and simple directions on the worksheets, correlations to other subjects in the day's curriculum, and overall manageability of the program.

How to Use *Let's Learn English* in an ESL Classroom

Program Design. This program consists of 30 lessons grouped into ten units. Each unit has three lessons related to the unit theme and teaches a specific essential reading skill. Units One through Five are intended for kindergarten through first grade. Units Six through Ten are designed for the older and/or more proficient ESL student.

The program design allows a teacher of second language learners the flexibility to select a unit of study by theme or by reading objective. The five themes are Me, Family, Food, Home, and School. The five reading objectives are Following Directions, Drawing Conclusions, Categorizing, Main Idea, and Sequence.

Lesson Format. Each lesson has an instructional delivery plan that is sequential, logical, and educationally sound. The six-step format includes Motivation, Activity, Explain/Model, Practice, (W)Rapping It Up, Extending Reading and Thinking.

Placement. Use a student's instructional reading level or language proficiency level for initial placement. Whether a student should be placed in the first five units or the last five units of study is best determined by a combination of teacher judgment and performance scores.

Grouping. This program lends itself well to either large group or small group instruction. A combination of grouping patterns may produce the most effective utilization of materials, time, and resources.

Scheduling. A classroom teacher of ESL who has a 20- to 30- minute block of time each day for supplemental language instruction should find that each lesson in *Let's Learn English* takes approximately one week to teach. Of course, scheduling will always vary depending on the skill needs, conceptual development, and language proficiency levels of specific students.

Acknowledgments

We would like to express our gratitude to our typist, Estela R. Flores, and we wish to thank our families for their support and patience. In closing, we especially want to thank the children of the Rio Grande Valley of Texas for having enriched our lives.

Unit One
ME

In this unit, children will use language as they relate to their own experiences about themselves. They will practice following directions, and they will learn the vocabulary for facial parts and motions.

Lesson One
LOOKING AT ME

Motivation

Students name and point to the parts of the face shown on the Theme Sheet.

Activity

Read the poem and have the children imitate your motions.

POEM

Looking at me. *(Cup hands around face.)*
What do I see? *(Place hand over eyes.)*
I see two eyes, one nose, one mouth. *(Point to each.)*
Looking at me, what else do I see? *(Cup hands around face.)*
On top of my eyes are two fuzzy eyebrows. *(Touch eyebrows.)*
I see two cheeks, a neck, a chin. *(Point to each.)*
White, pearly teeth that give a grin. *(Smile.)*
With hair on my head and ears to hear. *(Touch hair and ears.)*
I like my face from year to year. *(Cup hands around face.)*

Explain/Model

Teach students about following directions as you demonstrate these actions.

I/You (close) my/your (eyes). (pull) (ears)
I/You (wiggle) my/your (nose). (open) (mouth)
I/You (raise) my/your (eyebrows). (toss) (hair)
I/You (nod) my/your (head). (twist) (neck)
I/You wrinkle my/your face.
I/You chew with my/your teeth.
I/You stick out my/your chin.

Practice

Distribute Worksheet 1, LISTEN AND DO. Have the students follow your verbal directions. After they cut out the "X" and "O," tell them to put the letters on the facial parts you name. Then have each child draw an "X" or an "O" on one facial part you name.

(W)Rapping It Up

GAME

In order to play the game of "Picture Parts," you will need pictures of facial parts cut from magazines and a large paper bag. Each child reaches in the bag, takes out a picture, and identifies the part of the face. When all the pictures have been taken out and identified, tape them on posterboard or the chalkboard so that the parts form faces.

★ ★

Extending Reading and Thinking

★ *Have the children draw pictures of themselves, and display their self-portraits on a bulletin board. Then have them guess the identity of each picture. Later, you can mount the pictures in a class scrapbook entitled "Looking for Me."*

★ *For additional practice in following directions, tell the children to team up in pairs. Then have the partners take turns in giving verbal directions (such as "Close your eyes" or "Touch your nose") to one another.*

★ ★

Lesson Two
MIRROR, MIRROR

Motivation

Give the children simple directions as they review the parts of the face on Worksheet 1.

Activity

`SONG`

Sing the song "Mirror, Mirror" (to the tune of "Skip To My Lou"), substituting other phrases from Lesson One for the italicized phrase.

> *Mirror, Mirror*
> Mirror, mirror on the wall,
> Look at me I stand so tall,
> Touch your face and *close your eyes*,
> Mirror, mirror do as I say.

Explain/Model

Teach the children to follow two directions at the same time. Start by wiggling your nose and raising your eyebrows simultaneously. Then have the students do it. Use other facial motions covered in Lesson One to demonstrate further. In each case, have the children follow your directions.

Practice

Give the children Worksheet 2, PLEASE PUT ME TOGETHER. The children then practice following directions as you tell them what color(s) to use for each part, what parts to cut, and where to paste the cut-out parts.

Then give the children Worksheet 3, FINISH ME. Give them directions for completing the picture in a specific order.

(W)Rapping It Up

`EXPERIENCE CHART`

Have children tell you what they like about themselves, and write what they say on an "experience chart." Later, read the stories back to them.

★ ★

Extending Reading and Thinking

★ *Using an overhead projector, play the game "Face Race." Start by dividing a clear transparency into two sections. Then divide the class into two teams. Show a picture of a facial part, and have each team try to name it. The first team to name the part races to the overhead and draws it on the transparency. The team that draws a complete face first is the winner.*

★ *To do "Reflections," you will need to provide the children with hand mirrors. As you name each part of the face, the children touch that part. Then they team up and, using the mirrors, compare how their faces are like and unlike each other's.*

★ ★

Lesson Three
FUN FOR ME

Motivation

Review facial parts and their functions.

Activity

DISCUSSION

Have a discussion with the children about why their eyes are important. Ask them what they would do if they didn't have their eyes, mouth, etc.

Explain/Model

Use Worksheet 4, AT MY BIRTHDAY PARTY, to teach the parts of the face and their functions. Start by having the children look at each picture as you describe it. Then ask what facial part is being used. Finally, encourage the children to imitate the action in each picture.

Practice

Have the children do Worksheet 4, AT MY BIRTHDAY PARTY. Tell them to follow the directions on the worksheet.

Then have them do Worksheet 5, FUNNY FACE. Start with a review of following directions. Then tell the children what color to use for each part, what part to cut out, and where to paste it.

(W)Rapping It Up

GAME

Play the game "Pin the Part on the Face." This game is played just like "Pin the Tail on the Donkey" but with facial parts. You can use the parts on Worksheet 2 for this game.

★ ★

Extending Reading and Thinking

★ *Encourage children to bring photographs of themselves at different ages. Make a photo album and put it at an interest center.*

★ *Using paper plates or paper bags, children can make masks by attaching cutouts of facial parts from various art scraps.*

★ ★

Name _____

LOOKING AT ME

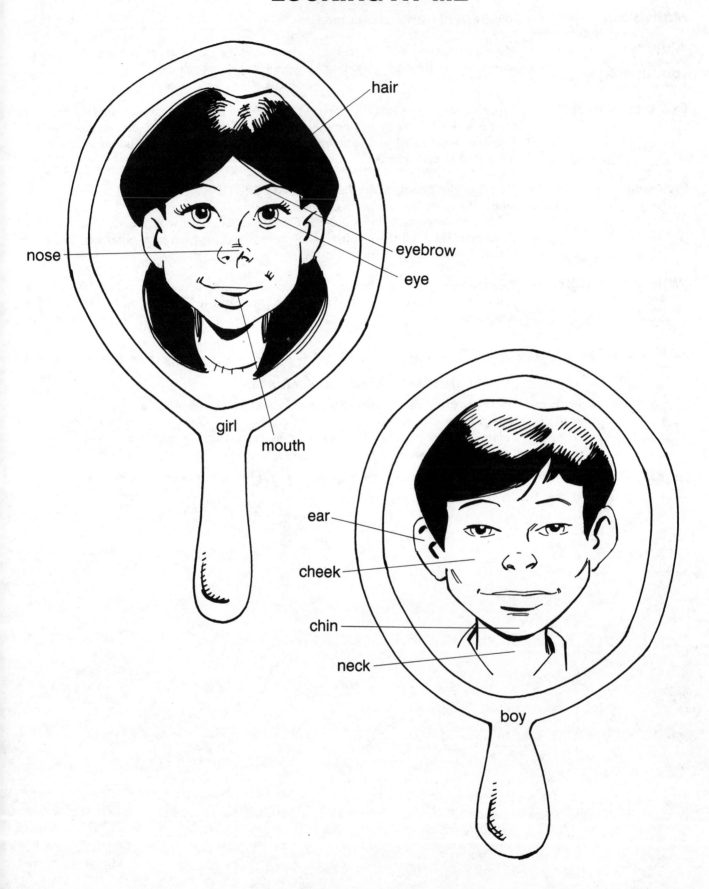

Name _____

LISTEN AND DO

Directions: Listen to your teacher and follow instructions. Cut out the X and the O. Put each letter where your teacher says on the face below.

Name _____

PLEASE PUT ME TOGETHER

Directions: Listen to your teacher and follow instructions. Color the face parts below. Then cut them out and paste the face together.

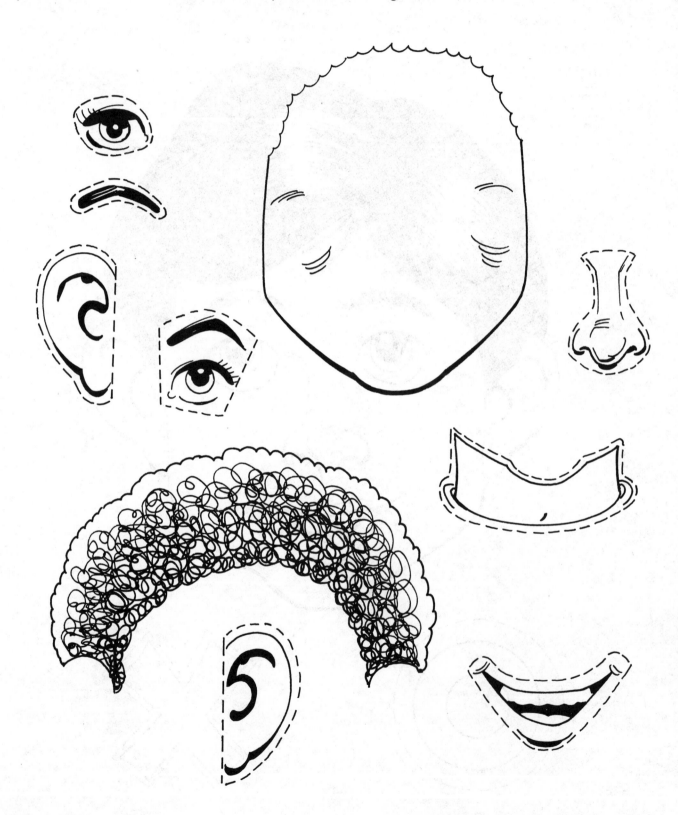

From *Let's Learn English: Second Language Activities for the Primary Grades*, Copyright © 1987 Scott, Foresman and Company.

Name _____

FINISH ME

Directions: Listen to your teacher and follow instructions. Finish the picture by drawing face parts in the order that your teacher says.

Name _____

AT MY BIRTHDAY PARTY

Directions: Cut out the boxes with the pictures of face parts at the bottom of the page. Paste each picture box under the drawing that shows the face part being used.

Name _____

FUNNY FACE

Directions: Do what your teacher says to make each face.

Unit Two
FAMILY

In this unit, children will use language as they relate to their own experiences about the family. They will learn the vocabulary for family and emotions, and they will practice drawing conclusions and using polite phrases.

Lesson One
FEELINGS

Motivation   Students name the family members shown on the Unit Two Theme Sheet.

Activity   Discuss what each family member is doing and how each one feels (angry, sad, etc.)

DISCUSSION

Explain/Model   Begin to teach students about drawing conclusions by discussing the pictures on the Theme Sheet. Discuss family activities such as shopping, working together, going for a drive, etc. List the emotions that family members may have felt as they participated in such activities. For example, "When Dad catches a fish, Dad is happy." Continue with all of the "photos."

Practice   Give the students Worksheet 1, A FAMILY TOGETHER. Then ask the following:

"Who is swimming in the lake?" (mother)
"Does she feel happy or sad?" (happy)
"Who is fishing?" (father and grandfather)
"Do they feel sad or glad?" (sad)

Continue until the students have named all the family members.

(W)Rapping It Up   Sing the song "Family Fun" (to the tune of "Twinkle, Twinkle Little Star").

SONG

Family Fun
Mother, Father, having fun,
At the lake out in the sun.
Brother, sister, out at play,
Oh, we've had a real good day.
Happy, angry, scared, and sad,
Family fun we all have had.

★ ★

Extending Reading and Thinking
★ *Have the children draw a picture of a family activity and label each family member.*
★ *Pantomime an emotion and see whether the children can guess the emotion.*
★ *Play the record "Peter and the Wolf" and ask students to identify the emotions they experience while listening.*

★ ★

Lesson Two
WORKING TOGETHER

Motivation

Discuss ways that a family can work together. Have each child draw a picture and label the family members in the work scene.

Activity

PANTOMIME

Place a box of old clothes and household props in the center of a circle of children. One child selects a prop and pretends to be a family member doing a job around the house. The other children guess who the family member is and what is happening.

Explain/Model

Continue teaching students about drawing conclusions. Start by pointing out to the children that in the pantomime they were able to use clues to figure out who the family member was and what was happening.

Give the children Worksheets 2 and 3—A FAMILY AT WORK. Tell the children to use the picture and story clues to find the answers to the questions on the worksheets. Do the first one with them to be sure they can identify the clues: vegetable garden, hoe, shovel. Continue by reading the three other family work situations. Assist with clues only if necessary.

Practice

Give the children Worksheet 4, FAMILY FUN. Read the directions aloud, and remind the children to listen for clues in the story that will help them answer the questions. Read each item of the story, and then allow them time to answer each question.

(W)Rapping It Up

CHANT

Read "Who Are You Going To Call?" with a quick rhythm. Snap your fingers as you read each stanza.

Who Are You Going To Call?

When you are sad and lonely
And you need to talk.
Who are you going to call?
Call your father!

When you are ill and weak
And you need to get well.
Who are you going to call?
Call your mother!

When you are tired and hungry
And you need to eat.
Who are you going to call?
Call your brother!

When you are happy and giggly
And you want to share a joke.
Who are you going to call?
Call your sister!

When you are working and alone
And you want to finish quick.
Who are you going to call?
Call your family!

★ ★

Extending Reading and Thinking

★ *List ways that students in the class help at home. The class can then compare lists and decide who helps the most.*

★ *Cut out magazine pictures of family members at work and play. Then have the children place the pictures appropriately on the bulletin board under the proper headings—WORK or PLAY.*

★ ★

Lesson Three
BEING POLITE

Motivation

List some polite words or phrases, and ask the children to name others. Discuss when and why people use these phrases.

Activity

ROLE PLAY

Have some children pretend to be a family eating lunch. Use props such as dishes, plastic foods, etc. Have the children use polite phrases such as "Pass the butter, please."

Explain/Model

Give the children Worksheet 5, THE POLITE PIG FAMILY. Tell the children that the pictures show the Polite Pig Family. Explain that each pig has a favorite way of being nice. Read the sentences at the bottom of the worksheet. Have the children repeat the polite phrases.

Practice

Have the children make the finger puppets shown on Worksheet 5, THE POLITE PIG FAMILY. Then describe each pig to the children. From the clues given, children put the corresponding puppet on their finger and recall the pig's favorite polite phrase.

(W)Rapping It Up

SONG

Sing the song "Mother's Pie" (to the tune of "Mary Had A Little Lamb").

Mother's Pie
Mother Piggy made a pie,
Nice and warm juicy pie.
Brother Piggy wants a piece,
Please say, "May I?"

Father Piggy ate some pie,
Nice and warm juicy pie.
It was really very good,
Please say, "Thank you."

Sister Piggy took some pie,
Nice and warm juicy pie.
Bumped into the baby's chair,
Please say, "Excuse me."

Baby Piggy dropped the pie,
Nice and warm juicy pie.
Hurry up and clean it up,
Please say, "I'm sorry."

★ ★

Extending Reading and Thinking

★ *Using the Polite Pig Family finger puppets, create a dialogue using polite phrases.*
★ *Use the polite phrases at the bottom of Worksheet 5 as sentence starters. Suggest a family scene such as cooking together, and have the children complete sentences about the scene.*

★ ★

Name _____

A FAMILY ALBUM

Name _____

A FAMILY TOGETHER

Directions: Listen to your teacher and answer the questions.

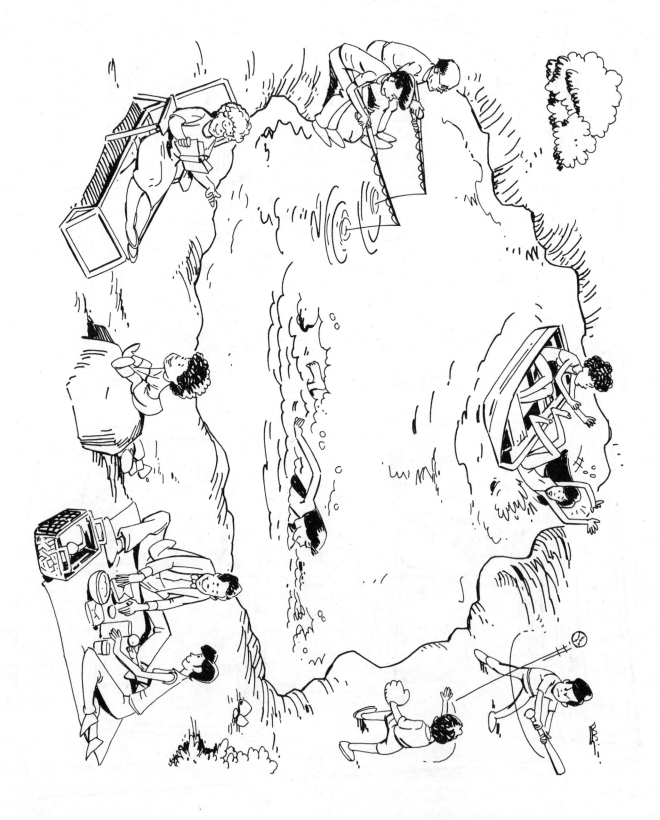

Name _____

A FAMILY AT WORK

Directions: Listen to your teacher read the sentences. Answer the questions and color the picture clues.

1. Mother is in the yard. She has a shovel and hoe. Is she hanging clothes or planting a garden?

2. Brother is in the garage. He has a garbage bag. Is he playing basketball or throwing out the trash?

K (continued)

Direction nces. Answer the
questions

3. apy water and a
ne plants?

4. Sister is riding her bike. She has a sack full of
newspapers on her bike. Is she delivering newspapers or
playing races?

Name _____

FAMILY FUN

Directions: Listen to your teacher read the story and the questions.
Trace over the word that tells the answer. Then color the correct picture.

1. Sara and her brother like to help their mom. Sara says,
   "Look at this messy kitchen! There is lots of work to do.
   Together we can finish fast and surprise Mom."
   Where are Sara and her brother?

Home

Movie

2. David got the broom. Sara washed the dishes. Together
   they cleaned and cleaned.
   What are Sara and David doing?

Working

Playing

Name _____

THE POLITE PIG FAMILY

Directions: Cut out each of the pig finger puppets. Then listen to your teacher. Use the clues your teacher gives to put on the correct finger puppet. Say what each piggy likes to say.

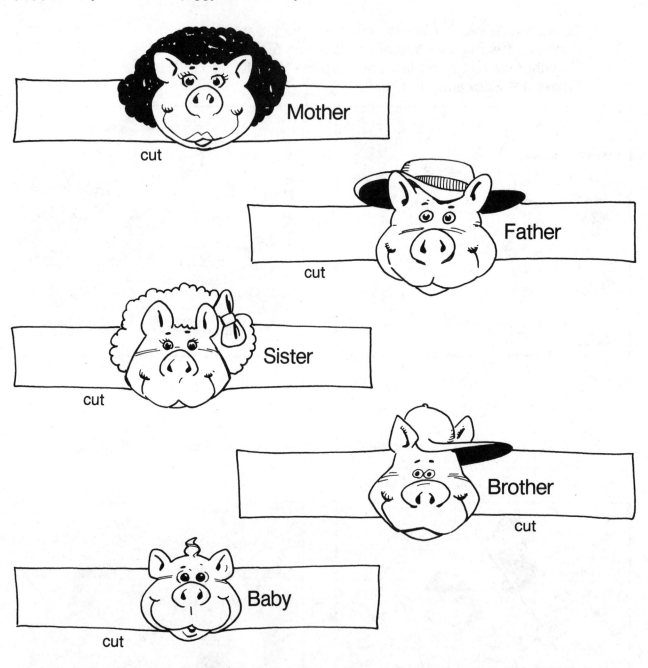

cut — Mother

cut — Father

cut — Sister

cut — Brother

cut — Baby

- -

(To be read by the teacher:)

When Mother wants some tea, Mother says, "Please."
When Father gets some pie, Father says, "Thank you."
When Brother wants to play, Brother says, "May I."
When Sister bumps the baby, Sister says, "Excuse me."
When Baby drops a dish, Baby says, "I'm sorry."

Unit Three
FOOD

In this unit, children will use language as they relate to their own experiences about food. They will practice classification skills and learn the vocabulary for fruits, vegetables, and breads.

Lesson One
FRUITS, VEGETABLES, AND BREADS

Motivation

Students name and discuss the foods shown on the Unit Three Theme Sheet.

Activity

RIDDLE

Read "A Tasty Treat" to the students and have them answer the questions.

A Tasty Treat
Home from school and to the kitchen I go,
To the kitchen I go to eat a treat.
Tasty treat! Tasty treat!
Tell me what tasty treat I will eat.
What is cool and white and sounds like silk? (milk)
What is red and shiny and sounds like dapple? (apple)
What is sweet and fruity and sounds like wham? (jam)
What is white or brown and sounds like head? (bread)
What is mashed or fried and sounds like tomato? (potato)

Explain/Model

Teach the classification of foods—fruits, vegetables, and breads—from the Unit Three Theme Sheet. Reinforce sentence patterns by having students classify each food as follows:

_____ is a vegetable.   _____ are vegetables.
_____ is a fruit.   _____ are fruits.
_____ is a bread.   _____ are breads.

Practice

Use Worksheet 1, WHAT FOODS GO TOGETHER? Have the children color and cut out the pictures of foods. Then have them cut out the words naming the foods. Finally, have the children paste each picture with its label under the correct group name on a separate sheet of paper.

(W)Rapping It Up

GAME

Play the game "Cool Foods." Prepare the game by creating a large refrigerator pocket chart. Label the pockets with the names of the food groups. Bring in pictures of vegetables, fruits, and breads, and have the children put the "foods" in the correct refrigerator pockets. You can extend the "Cool Foods" game by having the children match word cards to the pictured food items.

★ ★

Extending Reading and Thinking

★ *You can make a food collage by pasting pictures from magazines on posterboard.*
★ *Have the students research how certain foods grow. When they finish their research, have them classify the foods according to how they grow. Display the research findings in your science center.*

★ ★

Lesson Two
WE LOVE TO EAT

Motivation

Using the Unit Three Theme Sheet, students review items in the refrigerator.

Activity

| CHANT |

Teacher and student play "Who Likes . . .?"

Teacher: Who likes milk? (*Child's name*) likes milk.
Child: Who me? Yes, me. I like milk.
      (or)
Not me. I don't like milk.

Teacher: (*Child's name*) likes milk.
      (or)
(*Child's name*) doesn't like milk.

Repeat using the names of other students and other foods.

Explain/Model

Use the Unit Three Theme Sheet to have students classify foods into likes and dislikes. Teach the sentence patterns: Do you like _____ ? I don't like _____. I like _____. (*Child's name*) doesn't like _____.

Practice

Students draw foods they like and dislike on Worksheet 2, WHAT FOODS DO I LIKE? After completing the worksheet, children may discuss their likes and dislikes.
   On Worksheet 3—WHAT FOODS DO MY FRIENDS LIKE?—students write the names of three friends at the top and then indicate whether each friend likes or dislikes the foods pictured. After completing this worksheet, the children may report their findings.

(W)Rapping It Up

| PROJECT |

Grow a mini-garden in an egg carton. Before you plant seeds, discuss what foods the children like and dislike.

★ ★

Extending Reading and Thinking

★ *Take a poll to find out favorite fruits, vegetables, and breads. Then create a pictograph of the results. The children can then discuss which foods most of their classmates like best.*
★ *Read a simple menu from a fast-food restaurant (like Burger King or McDonald's), and discuss student likes and dislikes.*

★ ★

Lesson Three
A RAINBOW OF FOODS

Motivation

Students review colors and food.

Activity

| SONG |

Sing the song "What is Good to Eat?" (to the tune of "London Bridge").

What is red and good to eat?
What is red and is sweet?
What is red and good to eat?
Apples and strawberries.

What is yellow and good to eat?
What is yellow and a treat?
What is yellow and good to eat?
Cheese and butter.

What is white and good to eat?
What is white and is neat?
What is white and good to eat?
Milk and eggs.

Then chant:

Strawberries and apples are red. Milk and eggs are white. Cheese and butter are yellow. Tell me which ones you like (or don't like).

Explain/Model

Prepare cut-outs of baskets with the name of a color on each. Have the children classify foods into color categories by saying which foods should go in each basket. Reinforce sentence patterns:

_____ is a fruit.
It is red (green, yellow, etc.)
_____ and _____ are fruits.
They are red.

_____ is a vegetable.
It is red (green, yellow, etc.)
_____ and _____ are vegetables.
They are red.

Use the following questions to cue responses:

What *red* fruits *do* you like?
What *red* vegetables *do* you like?

What *red* fruits *don't* you like?
What *red* vegetables *don't* you like?

Practice

Give the students Worksheet 4, WHAT IS RED, WHITE, AND YELLOW? Have the children color and cut out the pictures of foods. Then have them cut out the words naming the foods. Finally, have the children paste each picture with its label under the correct color name on a separate sheet of paper.

(W)Rapping It Up

STORY

Read the story *Mr. Rabbit and the Lovely Present* by Charlotte Zolotow (N.Y.: Scholastic Book Services, 1962) to the children. The story is about a child who doesn't know what birthday gift to buy her mother. Mr. Rabbit suggests that she bring her mother a basket of fruit containing one fruit for each color of the rainbow. The illustrations by Maurice Sendak are extremely colorful.
Role play dialogue between the young girl and Mr. Rabbit.

★ ★

Extending Reading and Thinking

★ *Create an experience chart or simple poem in which you describe the colors as foods.*
Example: Red is a juicy apple.
         Green is a fat pear.
         Purple is a pretty grape.
★ *Bring a variety of foods to the class. Have the children guess which foods will leave a color stain when mashed between two pieces of paper. Mash the foods and label the stains by food used and color produced. Display the results at a science center.*

★ ★

Name _____

TASTY TREATS

Name _____

WHAT FOODS GO TOGETHER?

Directions: Color and cut out each food picture below. Then cut out the words that name the foods and the three food group names. Paste the food group names as headings on a separate sheet of paper. Then paste each food picture with its label under the correct heading.

Fruits	Vegetables	Breads
plums	crackers	corn
raisins	potatoes	bread

Name _____

WHAT FOODS DO I LIKE?

Directions: Draw the foods you like in the top of the refrigerator. Draw the foods you don't like in the bottom of the refrigerator.

I like:

I don't like:

Name _____

WHAT FOODS DO MY FRIENDS LIKE?

Directions: Write the first names of three friends in the top row. Ask each friend: "Do you like strawberries?" Check yes or no. "Do you like jam?" Check yes or no. "Do you like peanut butter?" Check yes or no.

	Friends		
Foods	**Name:**	**Name:**	**Name:**
	_____ yes _____ no	_____ yes _____ no	_____ yes _____ no
	_____ yes _____ no	_____ yes _____ no	_____ yes _____ no
	_____ yes _____ no	_____ yes _____ no	_____ yes _____ no

Name _____

WHAT IS RED, WHITE, AND YELLOW?

Directions: Color and cut out each food picture below. Then cut out the words that name the foods and the three food colors. Paste the food color words as headings on a separate sheet of paper. Then paste each food picture with its label under the correct heading.

Red	**White**	**Yellow**
cheese	strawberries	apples
eggs	butter	milk

Unit Four
HOME

In this unit, children will use language as they relate to their own experiences about the home. They will practice the skill of finding the main idea, learning vocabulary for opposites, and using pronouns.

Lesson One
PLAYING AT HOME

Motivation

Discuss the picture on the Unit Four Theme Sheet. Point to the children on the Theme Sheet as you sing the song below.

Activity

Sing the song "Going Over" (to the tune of "Are You Sleeping?").

SONG

> *Going Over*
> Going over, going over.
> Here I go, here I go.
> I am going over, I am going over,
> Come with me, come with me!

Continue by making up other verses using the vocabulary words on the Theme Sheet. Change the pronouns as necessary.

Explain/Model

Use the Unit Four Theme Sheet to teach the skill of finding the main idea. Point out that the details (chair, bed, a child going in a box, another going under a table, etc.) are parts of the main idea—fun at home. Ask questions ("Where are the children?" and "Are they having fun?") to elicit the main idea.

Practice

Have the children complete Worksheet 1, TOYS. Help the children understand that toys is the main idea of this worksheet by:

1. Listing the details (car, bridge, etc.)
2. Asking questions (What are these? Do you have fun with these?)

Then explain that the car can go over and under the bridge and right and left of the stop sign. The horse can go in and out of the barn. Sing "Going Over" again, this time using the vocabulary words on the Theme Sheet.

(W)Rapping It Up

MUSICAL

Stage a musical in which the children pretend to be a little car, trees, a bridge, a small hill, grandma's house, etc. Use the song "Going Over." Be imaginative and allow the children to express themselves creatively through dance and song.

★ ★

Extending Reading and Thinking

★ *After they perform the musical, the children can help capture the event on paper by telling what they did.*
★ *Have the children write a story about a little car going places on its journey home. Encourage them to use words that reinforce the "opposites" vocabulary.*

★ ★

Lesson Two
FUN WITH FRIENDS

Motivation

Use the Unit Four Theme Sheet to review activities that children are doing at home.

Activity

GAME

Play the game "Guess What I Am Doing." Like charades, the object of this game is to guess what someone is doing. Choose one child to draw a Unit Four Theme Sheet vocabulary word out of a box. The child should silently do whatever the word says. For example, s/he could crawl *under* a chair. The other children guess by saying, "S/he is going *under* the chair." Continue by having other children pantomime the other vocabulary words.

Explain/Model

Write on the chalkboard:

The childen are having fun. He is going over the table. She is going fast. The children are going in the box.

Tell the children that the underlined words are details that indicate the big idea of having fun.

Practice

Have the children complete Worksheet 2, THEY ARE GOING and Worksheet 3, FUN WITH CHAIRS. Read the directions with the children or have them work independently.

(W)Rapping It Up

ART

Provide graph paper and crayons for each child. Give the children directions for creating a design. For example, tell them to draw a blue box over a yellow one and then draw a purple box to the right of a green box, etc. Allow the students to create their own boxes and to talk about their designs when completed.

★ ★

Extending Reading and Thinking

★ *Read to the class from the* Sesame Street Up & Down Book. *This book of opposites teaches children that it is all right to have differences. "Different from" never means "inferior or superior to."*
★ *Make a chart of words with opposite meanings. Group the words under headings such as "Going Words"—stop/go, through/around, etc.; "Looking Words"—clean/dirty, pretty/ugly, big/small, same/different, etc.; "Feeling Words"—sad/happy, mad/glad, crying/laughing, etc.*

★ ★

Lesson Three
FUNNY FUN

Motivation

Have the children raise their right hands. Place a sticker on their right hand.

Activity

SONG

Sing "Hokey Pokey" and role play actions using the words right, left, in, and out.

Explain/Model

Teach the opposites of right and left. Start by drawing lines on the chalkboard to illustrate the directions. Vary the lines you draw, making some wavy, zigzag, dotted, etc. Then have the children practice going right and left in the air, on the chalkboard, or on their paper. To reinforce the main idea, write "Going right and left" at the top of your lines.

Practice

Have the children practice going right and left with their finger on Worksheet 4, BABY GOES TO MOM AND DAD. Ask them to name the picture after they complete the maze.

(W)Rapping It Up

PROJECT

Give each child a ball of dough. Tell the children to flatten the dough out like a pancake. Then help them press their right hand into the pancake. Insert a paper clip at the top of each pancake so that you can hang the imprinted circles of dough after leaving them to dry overnight. Be sure to write the child's name and the date on the back of each one. This can be a nice gift for Mom and Dad.

★ ★

Extending Reading and Thinking

★ *Using Worksheet 5—PUPPET PLAY—help the children cut and make stick puppets. Read the story starter on the worksheet, and allow the children to use the puppets creatively to complete the story. Encourage the use of the vocabulary for opposites and the sentence pattern "I am going . . . ."*

★ *Look for a book and tape called* Wee Sing *by Pamela Cown Beall and Susan H. Nipp (Price/Stern/Sloan, 1984). It's great for songs and fingerplays that promote language and awareness of left/right hands.*

★ ★

Name _____

HOME SWEET HOME

From *Let's Learn English: Second Language Activities for the Primary Grades*, Copyright © 1987 Scott, Foresman and Company.

Name _____

TOYS

Directions: Listen to your teacher and follow instructions.

Name _____

THEY ARE GOING

Directions: Cut out the boxes at the bottom of the page. Paste each box under the picture that shows what the words are saying.

| He is going up. | He is going down. |
| She is going out. | She is going in. |

Name _____

FUN WITH CHAIRS

Directions: Put an X on the children going over the chairs. Then draw a circle around the children going under the chairs. Use green to color the children who are going fast. Use yellow to color the children who are going slowly.

Name _____

BABY GOES TO MOM AND DAD

Directions: Use a blue color to show how Baby can find Dad. Use a red color to show how Baby can find Mom.

Name _____

PUPPET PLAY

Directions: Cut out the pictures of toys below and make them into stick puppets. Then listen to your teacher and finish the story.

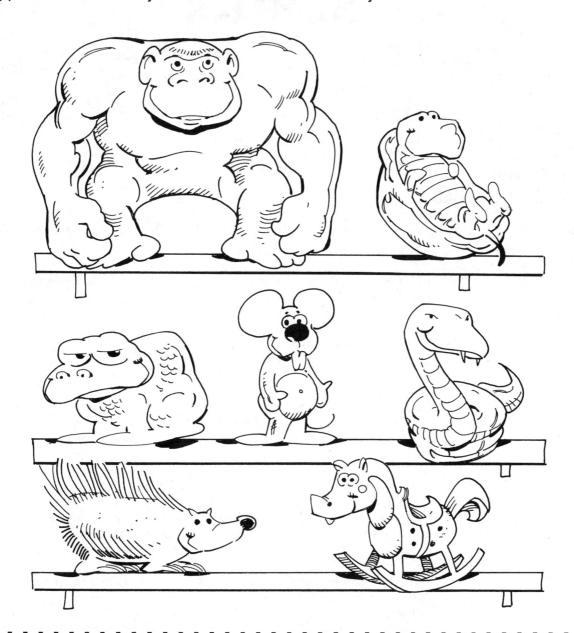

- -

(To be read by the teacher:)

    One night magic dust flew into the bedroom where the stuffed animals sat on the shelves. Magically, the toy animals came to life one by one.

    "Squeak!" said the mouse.

    "Ribit," croaked the frog.

    "S-s-s," hissed the snake.

    "Follow me," yelled the gorilla. And away they went into the night . . . .

Unit Five
SCHOOL

In this unit, children will use language as they relate to their own experiences about school. They will practice sequencing and will learn vocabulary relating to the school environment.

Lesson One
SCHOOL SUPPLIES

Motivation

Discuss the picture and name the school supplies shown on the Unit Five Theme Sheet.

Activity

CHANT

Put school supplies in a large paper bag. Have the children guess what school item they feel as they chant "Touch and Tell."

> *Touch and Tell*
> Touch and tell, touch and tell,
> See if your fingers can tell you well.
> I am touching a _____. (book, pencil, crayon, etc.)

Explain/Model

Teach sequencing by having the children listen to the following story and recall the order of events. Use the paper bag filled with school supplies to help tell the story. Then ask the children to tell you what Lizzie took out of the box first, second, third, etc.

> *Lizzie's School Box*
> Today is Lizzie's first day at school. She is very happy. She has a school box full of things to work with. (Pull out school box from bag.) In her school box she has a pencil to write with, some crayons to color, some scissors to cut out pictures, and some glue. Lizzie can hardly wait to use her school supplies.

Practice

Have the children complete Worksheets 1 and 2, LIZZIE'S SCHOOL SUPPLIES. Start by reviewing the school items on Worksheet 1. Then tell the children to listen to the continuation of the story "Lizzie's School Box." After listening to the story, the children will cut out pictures from Worksheet 1 and paste them in the correct order on Worksheet 2.

> *Lizzie's School Box*
> Mr. Lee is Lizzie's teacher. He says, "Take out your school box. I want you to use your pencil to draw a big apple on your paper." (Pause in order to let the children paste the first three items.) "Then color the apple red with your crayons. Cut out the apple with your scissors, and glue it on another sheet of paper."

(W)Rapping It Up

STORY

Have the children retell the story of "Lizzie's School Box." They may use the items from the paper sack.

Extending Reading and Thinking

★ *Encourage the children to tell each other a story using their school supplies. Have them recall what item was used first, second, etc.*

★ *Have a child describe a school item while the rest of the class tries to guess what it is. For example: "It is long, yellow, and pointed. What is it?" (pencil)*

★ ★

Lesson Two
ALL AROUND SCHOOL

Motivation   Introduce Worksheet 3, ALL AROUND SCHOOL, to the children.

Activity   Encourage the children to compare Lizzie's school as shown on the worksheet to their own school setting.

DISCUSSION

Explain/Model   Using Worksheet 3, tell the children to walk Lizzie through the different areas of the school as you name them. Make the activity story-like. Begin by saying:

1. Lizzie walks to school everyday.
2. In the morning she goes into her classroom.
3. Mr. Jones tells Lizzie to take the lunch money to the principal's office, etc.

Practice   Have the children practice sequencing by drawing a path as they recall Lizzie's day at school. After drawing the path, the children should number and color only those areas that Lizzie visited.

(W)Rapping It Up   Take a field trip around the school. Encourage the children to recall—in order—at least three different areas they visited.

FIELD TRIP

★ ★

Extending Reading and Thinking

★ *After the field trip, record the event on a chart tablet. Children may participate by telling what they saw and where they went. Use key words like first, next, and last to help the children recall the correct sequence.*

★ ★

Lesson Three
SCHOOL DAYS

Motivation   Using the Unit Five Theme Sheet, have the children locate the calendar and discuss the days of the week. Have them name the days they go to school and the days they spend at home.

Activity

SONG

Sing the song "Days of the Week" (to the tune of "Ten Little Indians").

Days of the Week
Monday, Tuesday we go to school,
Wednesday, Thursday you know the rule,
Here comes Friday let's be cool,
Saturday and Sunday there's no school.
Children come and say with me,
Seven days of the week:
Monday, Tuesday, Wednesday, Thursday,
Friday, Saturday, Sunday!

Explain/Model

Have the class do Worksheet 4, WE LIKE TO WORK AND PLAY. Make a set of seven copies of the worksheet for every child. In all of the sets, write the name of a different day of the week at the top of each sheet. Sing "Days of the Week." Then have the children draw their pictures about the day written at the top. Allow time for discussing each picture. Labeled pictures may be placed in plastic bags and displayed.

Practice

Have the children do Worksheet 5, SEVEN DAYS OF THE WEEK. When they finish, elicit discussion about what they do on different days of the week.

(W)Rapping It Up

GAME

Play the game "Musical Days of the Week." The game is played like musical chairs as the class sings "Days of the Week." Use seven chairs, and label each chair a different day of the week.

★ ★

Extending Reading and Thinking

★ *Using the student-drawn pictures from Worksheet 4, have the children write three descriptive sentences about each one.*

★ ★

Name _____

ABC AND 1-2-3

Name _____

LIZZIE'S SCHOOL SUPPLIES

Directions: Cut out the pictures of school supplies below. Paste them on Worksheet 2.

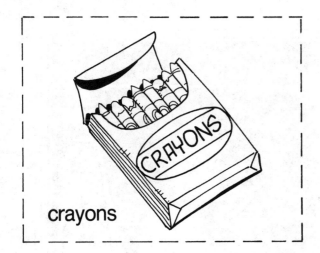

crayons

school box

glue

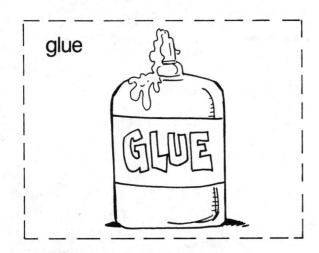

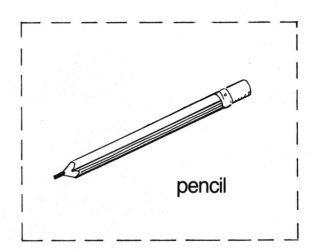

pencil

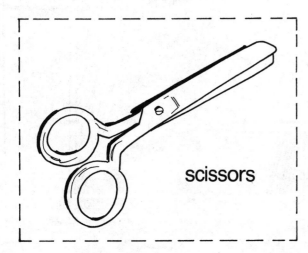

scissors

paper

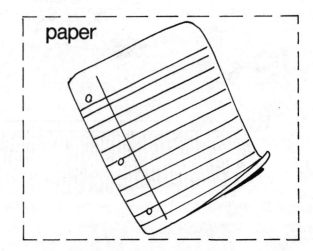

From *Let's Learn English: Second Language Activities for the Primary Grades*, Copyright © 1987 Scott, Foresman and Company.

Name _____

LIZZIE'S SCHOOL SUPPLIES (continued)

Directions: Listen to your teacher read the story "Lizzie's School Box."
Then paste the pictures from Worksheet 1 in the spaces below. Be sure to
put the pictures in the order they were read in the story.

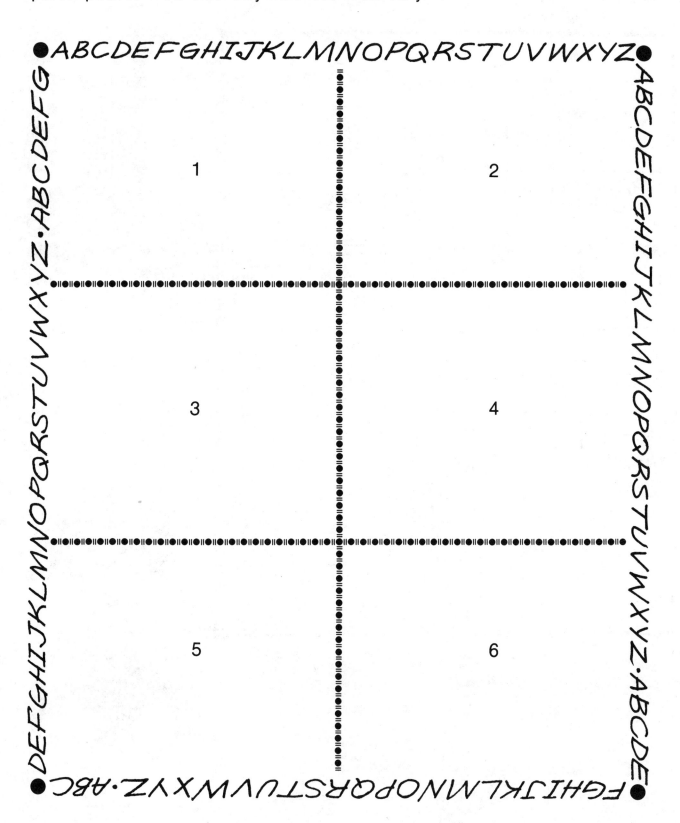

Name _____

ALL AROUND SCHOOL

Directions: Cut out the finger puppet. Then listen to your teacher and follow instructions. Walk Lizzie all around the school. Color only the areas that Lizzie visits.

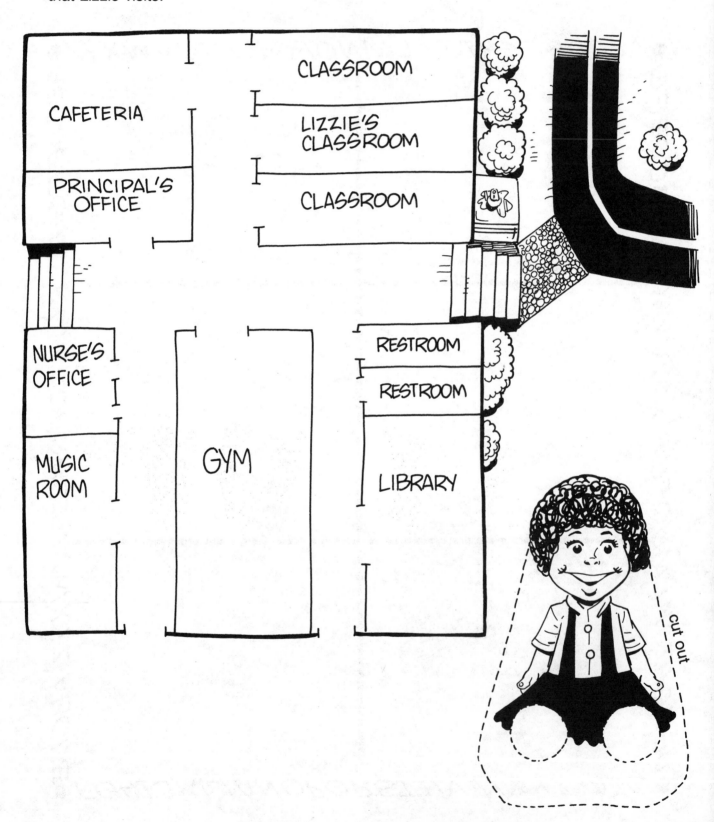

Name _____

WE LIKE TO WORK AND PLAY

Directions: Draw what you like to do on this day. Then tell about your pictures.

Day _____

Name _____

SEVEN DAYS OF THE WEEK

Directions: Cut out the boxes at the bottom of the page. Paste each box at the top of the page in the correct order for the days of the week. Trace over the numbers.

Tuesday	
Friday	
Thursday	
Sunday	
Wednesday	
Monday	
Saturday	

1	
2	
3	
4	
5	
6	
7	

From *Let's Learn English: Second Language Activities for the Primary Grades,* Copyright © 1987 Scott, Foresman and Company.

Unit Six
ME

In this unit, children will use language as they relate to their own experiences about themselves. They will practice following directions, learn self and body awareness, and use vocabulary words naming body parts and their motions.

Lesson One
THE CHANGING ME

Motivation

Discuss the changes from one photo to another shown on the Unit Six Theme Sheet.

Activity

FINGER PLAY

As you read "The Changing Me," have the children hold up one or more fingers to indicate age and act out the story line.

The Changing Me
As a one year old I played with my hands.
As a two year old I walked with my feet.
As a three year old I ate by myself.
As a four year old I brushed my teeth.
As a five year old I learned to write.
As a six year old I read a book.
As a seven year old I rode my bike.
And now at eight I am able to cook.

Explain/Model

Explain that each line in the finger play demonstrates an action. Continue by saying that there are groups of words that do not involve action. Ask the children for examples of phrases that show action and for phrases that do not show action. Give the children directives mixed with non-directive words or phrases. The children should role play action from the directives but remain still when the non-directive words/phrases are stated.

Practice

Have the children do Worksheet 1 and Worksheet 2, I CAN DO IT, I CAN, I CAN. Help the children understand that the actions shown on Worksheet 1 relate to actions they are able to do now that they are older. Have them follow the directions on the worksheet.

(W)Rapping It Up

GAME

In the game "Command-Do," a variation of the game "Simon Says," the leader gives directives and non-directives. Players participate by either acting out the commands (directives) or standing still in response to the non-directive statements.

★ ★

Extending Reading and Thinking

★ *Have the children cut out pictures from magazines of things they are able to do by themselves. They can then paste the pictures on sheets of paper and compile an "I Can" booklet. Encourage them to label the things they can do in their "I Can" booklets (swim, read a book, skate, etc.).*

★ *Have the children list five things they can do and five things they cannot do.*

★ ★

Lesson Two
THINGS I LIKE TO DO

Motivation

Discuss the activities shown on the Unit Six Theme Sheet. List those activities as well as others that children like to do.

Activity

PANTOMIME

Have the children take turns selecting things they like to do from the list of activities. Each child then pantomimes the action while the class tries to guess the activity.

Explain/Model

Teach children to follow written directions. Start by writing the following sentences on the chalkboard:

a. I like to sing.
b. *Clap your hands.*
c. I like to play with my pet.
d. *Write your pet's name.*
e. I like to eat hamburgers.
f. *Tell a friend your favorite hamburger place.*

Explain that sentences a, c, and e are things they like to do. Sentences b, d, and f give directions. Model sentences a-d. Have the children do sentences e and f.

Distribute Worksheet 3, THE LAND OF THINGS I LIKE TO DO, and do two or three examples together.

Practice

Have the children practice following written directions on Worksheet 4, TELL ME SQUARES.

(W)Rapping It Up

SONG

Sing the song "If You're Happy and You Know It."

★ ★

Extending Reading and Thinking

★ *Encourage the children to give new directions in the song "If You're Happy . . ." by changing the things they like to do. For example, "If you're happy and you know it swim with me (ride your bike, fly a kite)."*

★ ★

Lesson Three
MY FAVORITE THINGS

Motivation

Have the children discuss all the pictures on Worksheet 5, MY FAVORITE THINGS, and name their favorite things. If their favorite thing is not shown, have them draw it in the blank space on the worksheet.

Activity

CHANT

Read the following chant, "My Favorite Things," with a quick rhythm.

My Favorite Things
_____ and _____ are my favorite things.
These are a few of my favorite things.
Tell me (*name of child*) your favorite things.

Explain/Model   Distribute Worksheet 6, TOOLS FOR FOLLOWING DIRECTIONS. Then write the
following worksheet directions on the chalkboard:

Put the **X** on the _____ .

Put the ▬ under the _____ .

Put the ■ or ● around the _____ .

Put the ➡ pointing to the _____ .

Put the ∿ over the _____ .

Put the ☺ or ☹ between the _____ and _____ .

Make transparencies of Worksheets 5 and 6. Read the first two sentences from the
chalkboard aloud, and—using the overhead projector and the transparencies—show
the children how to use the tools for following directions. Have the children take
turns reading the directions from the chalkboard as you continue to demonstrate the
procedure.

Practice   Have the children copy the sentences from the chalkboard, filling in the blanks with
words they find on Worksheet 5, MY FAVORITE THINGS. Then have them
exchange papers with a partner. The partners then follow directions, using the tools
from Worksheet 6.

(W)Rapping It Up   Have the children cut out pictures of their favorite things and make a booklet titled
"My Favorite Things."

| BOOKLET |

★ ★

Extending Reading and Thinking

★ *Using their "My Favorite Things" booklet, the children can label the pictures.*
Encourage them to write a sentence about each favorite thing.
★ *The children may bring favorite items of interest from home to add to an interest*
center. A tape recorder placed at the center will allow children to record their names, the
items they brought in, and why they like them. Replay the tape for the class to enjoy.

★ ★

Name _____

THE CHANGING ME

Name _____

I CAN DO IT, I CAN, I CAN

Directions: Cut out the pictures below that show action that children can do. Paste the pictures on Worksheet 2.

Directions: Cut out the boxes below that have sentences that give a command of what children can do. Paste these sentences on Worksheet 2.

Her hair is long.	Color the picture.
Jump up and down.	Close your eyes.
Draw a big square.	That is my dog.
Raise your hand.	Count to twenty.

Name _____

I CAN DO IT, I CAN, I CAN (continued)

Directions: Paste the pictures and sentences from Worksheet 1 below.

From *Let's Learn English: Second Language Activities for the Primary Grades,* Copyright © 1987 Scott, Foresman and Company.

Name _____

THE LAND OF THINGS I LIKE TO DO

Directions: Follow the trail from Start to Finish. Read each sentence and do the underlined activity as you move from space to space.

Start		
I like to read a book. <u>Find the book on this sheet and color it blue.</u>	I like to ride my bike. <u>Clap two times.</u>	I like to watch TV. <u>Write the name of your favorite TV show in the next square.</u>
		_____ _____ _____
I like to go swimming. <u>Find the swimming pool on this sheet and color it.</u>	I like to eat hamburgers. <u>Rub your tummy.</u>	I like to see good movies. <u>Jump up and down.</u>
I like to do my homework. <u>Raise your right hand in the air.</u>		**Finish**
I like to color. <u>Go back and color the squares of things that are your favorite things to do.</u>	I like to play video games. <u>Tell your friend the name of your favorite video game.</u>	I like to dance. <u>Stand up and take a bow.</u>

From *Let's Learn English: Second Language Activities for the Primary Grades*, Copyright © 1987 Scott, Foresman and Company.

51

Name _____

TELL ME SQUARES

Directions: You will need some paper, a pencil, and a pair of dice for this activity. Roll the dice and add the two numbers that come up. Then look at the square below that has the same number that you rolled with the dice. Do what the square says.

Take turns with your friends. If anyone rolls the same number more than once, that person should roll again.

2 Write your name on your paper.	**3** Stand up and touch your toes.	**4** Draw a picture of yourself.
5 Write the two things you like to do best.	**6** Touch your eyes, nose, mouth, and ears.	**7** Draw a birthday cake with the right number of candles to show how old you are.
8 Wave goodbye to your teacher.	**9** Open your reading book and write three 'b' words on your paper.	**10** Write the names of your three favorite toys.
11 Write the day of the week.	**12** Write the time of day that your favorite TV show comes on.	Did you finish every square?

Name _____

MY FAVORITE THINGS

Directions: Listen to your teacher and follow instructions, using the figures on Worksheet 6.

swing

records

football

video game

dog

doll

book

cat

bicycle

TV

guitar

cars

radio

baseball

pillow

Name _____

TOOLS FOR FOLLOWING DIRECTIONS

Directions: Cut out each of the figures below. Then listen to your teacher and follow instructions, using the figures on Worksheet 5.

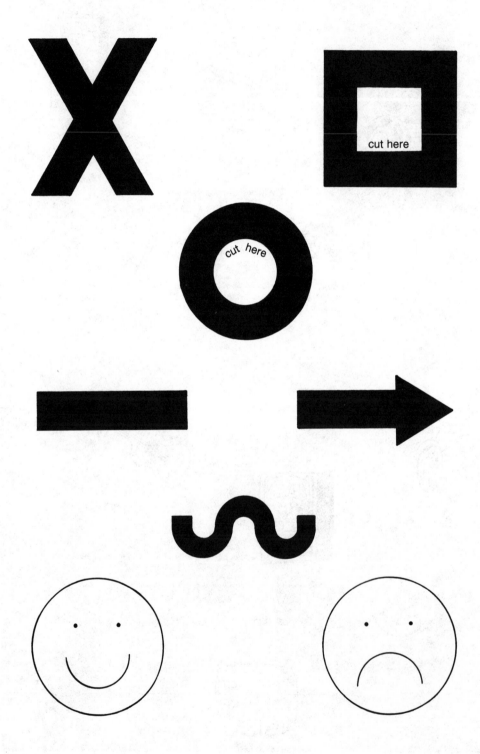

Unit Seven
FAMILY

In this unit, children will use language as they relate to their own experiences about the family. They will practice drawing conclusions and will learn vocabulary relating to family needs.

Lesson One
GOING TO THE MALL

Motivation

Discuss the picture on the Unit Seven Theme Sheet. Encourage the children to talk about family experiences at a mall or shopping center. Make a list of items the children and their families recently bought at a mall.

Activity

SONG AND DANCE

Have the children act out the lyrics while you sing "Going To The Mall" (to the tune of "Bunny Hop").

> *Going To The Mall*
> We're going to the mall,
> We're going to have some fun,
> Riding in the car—bump, bump, bump.
>
> We're at the parking lot,
> Come on let's all get out,
> We're going to buy something—shop, shop, shop.
>
> Walking down the mall,
> Store after store,
> We're all getting hungry—munch, munch, munch.

Talk about the different types of stores presented on the Theme Sheet. Discuss what items are sold in the different shops. Then model and practice the following patterns:

Mom needs *shoes*. She will go to the *shoe shop*.
Dad needs *some pants*. He will go to the *men's shop*.

Repeat using different family members, different needs, and different stores.

Practice

Have the students complete Worksheet 1, SHOPPING. After finishing the worksheet, the children may enjoy a choral reading of the story.

(W)Rapping It Up

ROLE PLAY

Pretend to be a family shopping at a mall. Role play a dialogue—"Where To Buy" or "What I Need."

Extending Reading and Thinking

★ Bring in or draw a map of a shopping mall. Have the children locate or draw different stores.

★ Cut out the illustrations on Worksheet 1 and paste them on a blank sheet of paper. Have the children label the illustrations and draw others.

Lesson Two
EATING AT A MALL

Motivation

Have the children locate the restaurants on the Unit Seven Theme Sheet. Discuss what foods they enjoy eating at a mall.

Activity

DRAWING

Have the children fold a sheet of paper into four parts. On each part they should draw and label a favorite food they eat at a mall.

Explain/Model

Distribute Worksheet 2, WHERE TO EAT. Have the children read the story and follow the directions on the worksheet. (Answers may vary. The children should explain their choices.)

Practice

Distribute Worksheet 3, CHOOSE THE ONE, and have the children follow the directions on the worksheet.

(W)Rapping It Up

GROUP GAME

Distribute Worksheet 4, MAKE A LUNCH. The children play the game by placing the food squares on the game board in any order. Then they decide as a group what lunch is to be made (tacos, hamburger, pizza, or sandwich). As the teacher calls a number, the children take the food square off the same numbered board space *only* if that food square can be used to make the lunch. The winner is the child who completes the predetermined lunch item first.

Extending Reading and Thinking

★ Have the children write a menu, listing the prices for each food item. Let the children order an imaginary lunch from the food menu. They can choose any items they want, but the lunch must cost no more than $3.00.

★ Encourage a child to write a paragraph describing how to prepare hot dogs, spaghetti, etc., without actually naming the food item. Have another child read the paragraph and try to guess what the food is.

Lesson Three
FINDING HELP

Motivation

Have the children pretend to be a family on a shopping trip. While shopping, a child gets lost.

Activity	Lead a class discussion about a child getting lost during a visit to a shopping mall. What would the family do? How would they find help? What could the lost child do? How could the lost child find help?
DISCUSSION	

Explain/Model Distribute Worksheet 5, FINDING HELP. Do the first item together with the children. Remind them to use story clues to help them draw a conclusion and answer the questions.

Practice Distribute Worksheet 6, LOST! WHAT TO DO/LOST! WHAT TO SAY. Tell the children that this worksheet lists different things that Rita can do and say to find her family. Have them follow the worksheet directions to indicate what Rita should do and say. (Answers: a, d, f, g, j).

(W)Rapping It Up The children can create their own I.D. cards. Each identification card should include the following: picture, name, age, sex, address (including city and state), parent's name, and phone number. Review this information so that each child is able to recite it from memory.

WRITING

★ ★

Extending Reading and Thinking

★ *The children can do an art project that includes their thumb prints. Start by having them draw a tree. Tell them to create the leaves for the tree by pressing their thumbs first on a sponge soaked with green paint and then on the paper. The children should take their art projects home and tell their parents to save them for identification.*

★ *This would be a good time to extend the children's knowledge of ways to prevent being kidnapped. Tell the children to scream as loud as they can if they are ever taken by someone they don't know. Review other safety rules, such as not being fooled by a stranger offering candy, etc.*

★ ★

From *Let's Learn English: Second Language Activities for the Primary Grades*, Copyright © 1987 Scott, Foresman and Company.

Name _____

A FAMILY SHOPS

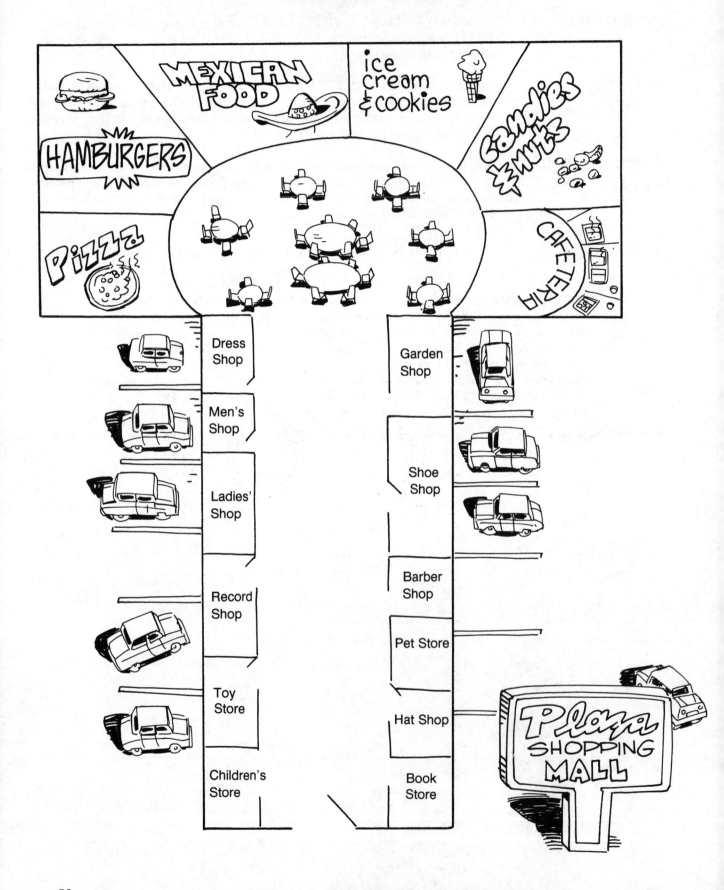

Name _____

SHOPPING

Directions: Read the story. Then cut out the boxes at the bottom of the
page. Put each box in its correct space so that the story makes sense.

A family goes to the mall one fine afternoon. Everyone needs to buy
something.

Dad needs a   and a   .

Does Dad go to the   ?

Oh, no, no, no! Dad will go to the   .

Mother needs   and a   .

Does Mother go to a   ?

Oh, no, no, no! Mother will go to the   .

Brother needs   and   .

Does Brother go to a   ?

Oh, no, no, no! Brother will go to the   .

Men's Shop	Garden Shop	Shoe Shop

Name _____

WHERE TO EAT

Directions: Read the story. Then answer the question at the bottom of the page. Circle the correct answer.

"It is time to eat. The children are hungry and I am too,"

said Mother.

Father said, "Children, what would you like to eat? We

need to decide where to go."

"I want to eat with ," said Tina.

"Oh, not I," said Rene. "I want to eat a

with ."

"Oh, not I," said Mother. "I want to eat

with ."

Then Dad asked, "Does anyone want to eat  with

me?"

Question: Where will the family eat?

Hamburger Stand

1

Pizza Parlor

2

Cafeteria

3

Name _____

CHOOSE THE ONE

Directions: Read about the foods that each member of the family likes to eat. Then draw circles around the pictures that answer the questions.

soup

cookies

1. Tina wants to eat something cool. She likes to eat it in a cone. Her favorite flavor is strawberry. What does Tina want to eat?

ice cream

crackers

pizza

2. Rene wants to eat something square and crunchy. He likes to eat it with peanut butter. What does Rene want to eat?

apple

banana

grapes

3. Mom and Dad want to eat some fruit. They like to eat this fruit with cereal. They peel the fruit and slice it before they eat it. What do Mom and Dad want to eat?

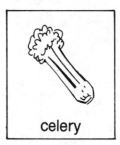
celery

Name _____

MAKE A LUNCH

Directions: Cut out the food squares. Place them in any order on the game board. Then listen to your teacher and follow instructions.

lettuce	tomato sauce	hamburger buns	taco shells	tomatoes	cheese

mayonnaise

ground beef

pepperoni

pickles

mustard

meat patty

1	2	3	4
5	6	7	8
9	10	11	12
13	14	15	16
17	18	19	20

Name _____

FINDING HELP

Directions: Read the story. Then underline the picture that answers each question.

1. Rita and her family went shopping. Rita saw some toys she liked. She ran to see them. When she turned around, her mother and father were gone! Her brother and sister were gone too! Rita knows her full name, phone number, and the names of her father and mother. What can Rita do to find help?

2. Rita's family cannot find her. They look and look in all the stores. Mom and Lisa go one way. Dad and Toni go another. No one finds Rita. Mom and Dad remember what clothes Rita is wearing. Mom has a picture of Rita in her purse. What can the family do to find help?

Name _____

LOST! WHAT TO DO

Directions: Read all of the sentences below. Circle the letter next to every sentence that will help Rita find her family.

a. Ask a sales clerk for help.

b. Begin to run home very fast.

c. Sit on the floor and play a game.

d. Look for a policeman.

e. Count from 1 to 100.

- -

LOST! WHAT TO SAY

Directions: Read all of the sentences below. Circle the letter next to every sentence that will help the policewoman find Rita's family.

f. "I am lost. Please help me!"

g. "My name is Rita Martin."

h. "Buy me some ice cream."

i. "I am a girl."

j. "My father's name is Daniel Martin."

Unit Eight
FOOD

In this unit, children will use language as they relate to their own experiences about food. They will practice classification skills, learn the Basic Four Food Groups, and use vocabulary for food.

Lesson One
BASIC FOUR

Motivation

Distribute the Unit Eight Theme Sheet, and encourage the children to talk about the picture and their experiences with family picnics. Name the foods shown on the Theme Sheet.

Activity

SONG

Sing the song "This is the Way" (to the tune of "Mulberry Bush"). Ham it up. Make it fun.

This is the Way
This is the way we peel bananas, peel bananas, peel bananas.
(Repeat)
On our family picnic.

This is the way we cut the onions . . . .
(Pretend to be crying as you cut.)

This is the way we make tortillas . . . .
(Pat hands together.)

Repeat using all of the foods on the Theme Sheet.

Explain/Model

Use the Theme Sheet to explain the Basic Four Food Groups. Organize foods from the table into the labeled grocery bags. Explain that "Meat" and "Dairy" products come from animals and that "Produce" and "Bread" products come from plants.

Practice

Have the children follow the directions and complete Worksheet 1, CHOOSING THE GROUP NAME. If necessary, explain that the group names may be other than the Basic Four. Give examples. Then distribute Worksheet 2, ANIMAL OR PLANT. Guide the children as they determine what foods come from animals and what foods come from plants.

(W)Rapping It Up

GAME

Play the game "What Am I?" To start, a child stands behind a picture, cut out and mounted, of a food. The picture should have a hole just big enough for the child to look through. The child—not knowing what the picture is—asks, "What Am I?" Others in the class describe the food and give hints, including the name of the Basic Four category, until the child guesses the food pictured.

★ ★

Extending Reading and Thinking

★ *Collect real foods and place them in a bag. Have the children reach in the bag, touch a food, and then try to name both the food and its Basic Four category.*

★ ★

From *Let's Learn English: Second Language Activities for the Primary Grades,* Copyright © 1987 Scott, Foresman and Company.

Lesson Two
FOOD AND THE FIVE SENSES

Motivation
Use the Unit Eight Theme Sheet to review the items on the picnic table and how they can be grouped into the Basic Four groups. Discuss the five senses as they relate to a food.

Activity
ROLE PLAY
Have the children pretend that they are a family of raccoons (or bears) and that they find the foods pictured on the Theme Sheet. Encourage them to use their five senses to explore each food thoroughly, reacting to appearance, odor, feel, taste, and sound.

Explain/Model
Model and elicit children's responses using all five senses. For example, "I like to smell _____ , _____ , _____ , and _____." "I don't like to hear _____ , _____ , _____ , and _____."

Practice
Have the children complete Worksheet 3, WHAT I LIKE and Worksheet 4, WHAT I DON'T LIKE. Then have them classify foods, using the food words presented on the Theme Sheet.

(W)Rapping It Up
EXPERIENCE
Bring some real food to the classroom. Encourage the children to experience the food with all five senses. Elicit discussion from the children along the lines of "I like to smell . . . ." (etc.); "I don't like to smell . . . ." (etc.).

★ ★

Extending Reading and Thinking

★ *Work with the children to compile a list of "The World's Most Beautiful Foods" or "The World's Noisiest Foods." (Continue with "Worst Looking," "Smelliest," "Worst Tasting.")*

★ *Have the children write a paragraph about the real food experience. Remind them to include descriptive words that tell how their five senses reacted to the food.*

★ ★

Lesson Three
DAILY MENU

Motivation
Discuss how foods from the Basic Four groups can be combined to create nutritious meals.

Activity
GAME
Label four paper bags "Bread," "Produce," "Meat," and "Dairy." Place the bags in front of the children. Ask what foods could be in each bag.
   Then play the game "What's Missing?" Have the children close their eyes. Remove one of the bags. When the children open their eyes, they try to name the missing bag.

Explain/Model   Write the word "Breakfast" on the chalkboard. Explain that you are going to serve a nutritious morning meal by fixing something from each food group. Model how you would consider items from each food group—e.g., "I like to eat _____ for breakfast." Repeat the process for lunch and dinner.

Practice   Have the children complete Worksheet 5, MAKING BREAKFAST and Worksheet 6, MENU. Tell the children to use foods from all the Basic Four Food Groups when preparing the menus for Worksheet 6.

(W)Rapping It Up   Read the story *The Very Hungry Caterpillar* by Eric Carle (Collins World, 1970). A
[STORY]   story that is sure to delight children of all ages, it follows the furry caterpillar as he eats his way through the days of the week.

★ ★

Extending Reading and Thinking

★ *Find poems about food and read them to the children. Help them enjoy the rhythm and rhymes of the English language.*

★ *Show the children how to write a haiku. Although usually about nature, haiku poems can be about food, too. Haiku poems do not have to rhyme; they simply must follow a 5-7-5 syllable pattern. For example:*

Munch, munch, munch a bunch   (5)
Of carrots and celery . . .   (7)
A food symphony!   (5)

★ ★

Name _____

EAT RIGHT—STAY FIT

chicken
bananas
yogurt
hamburger
carrots
onions
tortillas
celery
buns
tomatoes
steaks
COTTAGE CHEESE

Bread   **Produce**   **Meat**   **Dairy**

Name _____

CHOOSING THE GROUP NAME

Directions: Circle the one word in each group that is the group name for all the others.

chicken	milk
meat	cheese
hamburger	yogurt
steak	dairy
buns	onions
tortillas	carrots
bread	produce
crackers	tomatoes
bananas	potatoes
apples	vegetables
raisins	corn
fruit	celery
eggs	red food
white food	strawberries
milk	tomatoes
cottage cheese	apples

Name _____

ANIMAL OR PLANT

Directions: Write the names of foods that come from animals in the space at the top half of the page. Then write the names of foods that come from plants in the space at the bottom half of the page.

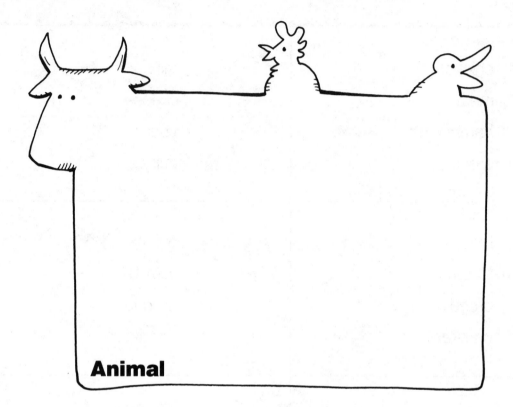

Animal

Plant

Name _____

WHAT I LIKE

Directions: Write the names of foods that you like to see, hear, smell, touch, and taste. Pay attention to the lines drawn from each set of lines to the child's eyes, ears, nose, hand, and mouth. Be sure to put each food name in the correct list.

_____   _____

_____   _____

_____   _____

_____   _____

_____   _____

_____   _____

_____   _____

_____   _____

_____

_____

_____

_____

_____

Name _____

WHAT I DON'T LIKE

Directions: Write the names of foods that you *don't* like to see, hear, smell, touch, and taste. Pay attention to the lines drawn from each set of lines to the child's eyes, ears, nose, hand, and mouth. Be sure to put each food name in the correct list.

_____   _____

_____   _____

_____   _____

_____   _____

_____   _____

_____   _____

_____   _____

_____   _____

_____

_____

_____

_____

Name _____

MAKING BREAKFAST

Directions: Read the story. Then fill in the blanks at the bottom of the page.

One day my mother told me to make breakfast. I went to the

. I opened the _____ . I took out the _____ ,

the _____ , the _____ , and the _____ .

"Something is missing," I thought to myself. The four basic food groups

are _____ , _____ , _____ ,

and _____ . I need some _____ .

Name _____

MENU

Directions: Plan and write three menus: one for breakfast, one for lunch, and one for dinner. Be sure to use foods from the four basic food groups in each menu.

Breakfast Menu

_____

_____

_____

_____

_____

_____

Lunch Menu

_____

_____

_____

_____

_____

_____

Dinner Menu

_____

_____

_____

_____

_____

_____

Unit Nine
HOME

In this unit, children will use language as they relate to their own experiences about the home. They will practice the skill of finding the main idea, learn about basic human needs, and use vocabulary words relating to the home.

Lesson One
MY HOME

Motivation

Name and point to the rooms of the house and the pieces of furniture shown on the Unit Nine Theme Sheet. Discuss the picture.

Activity

STORY

Distribute Worksheet 1, A TEENY TINY BOOK, and read the story to the children.

Explain/Model

Discuss the basic needs listed on the Theme Sheet. Explain why these needs are basic to our survival. Create a contrast by listing "wants" as opposed to "needs." Reread the story on Worksheet 1 and ask the children to identify the family's needs.

Practice

Have the children complete Worksheet 1, A TEENY TINY BOOK, by making the pages into a booklet that they can take home.

Then distribute Worksheet 2, THE SAD HOUSE STORY. Ask the children to retell the story of the sad house with the help of the pictures. They can cut out the pictures and add them to the booklets they made from Worksheet 1.

With Worksheet 3, AT HOME, the children should first identify rooms of the house. Then they should follow directions for writing the sentences.

(W)Rapping It Up

GAME

Play the game "Going on a Vacation," using a real suitcase filled with objects that a traveler would need when going away from home (e.g., box of cereal, powdered milk, blanket, wash cloth, toothbrush, sweater). Have each child pick an item from the suitcase and say, "I am going to _____ (sleep, eat, drink, etc.) on my vacation so I need a _____ ."

★ ★

Extending Reading and Thinking

★ *Try three different storytelling techniques: (a) teacher starts a story and children finish it; (b) children start a story and teacher ends it; and (c) each child contributes some part to a story.*

★ *Cut the story booklets into different shapes (trees, flowers, animals, etc.), and have the children write a story about the topic that each shape suggests.*

★ ★

Lesson Two
WHAT HAS WALLS, DOORS, AND A ROOF?

Motivation

Review the furniture and rooms of the house shown on the Theme Sheet.

Activity	Ask the following riddles:
RIDDLES	

What is warm on the outside, cold on the inside, and holds food? (a refrigerator)

What is long, soft, and holds people when they are sleepy? (a bed)

What can be any shape but always looks like you when you look at it? (a mirror)

What holds water and people when they want to wash? (a bathtub)

What has a back and four legs but doesn't walk? (a chair)

What shows people, places, and animals when it is on but shows nothing when it is off? (a TV)

What opens, closes, and can be locked? (a door)

What can be turned off in the daytime and on at night? (a lamp)

What is good for sitting on or laying on but not for jumping on? (a sofa)

Explain/Model

Teach the skill of determining the main idea of something. Tell the children to look for the key words in the riddles. For example, the key words long, soft, and sleepy suggest the answer—bed. Point out other key words that suggest the main idea of each riddle.

Practice

Distribute Worksheet 4, WHERE DOES IT GO? Have the children practice using key words such as stove, refrigerator, and table to suggest the main idea of kitchen. Then have them follow the directions on the worksheet.

(W)Rapping It Up

COLLECTIONS

Create a homework assignment. Ask each child to bring a collection of something—rocks, stamps, coins, leaves, flowers, books, tools, etc. Tell them to put their collections in a bag or box and to label the container with the name of the collection. This assignment not only provides a great opportunity to share interests, but it also helps the children focus on the main idea and expand their language skills.

★ ★

Extending Reading and Thinking

★ *Children love to read and ask each other all kinds of riddles. Collect riddle books so that they can have fun while increasing their reading and language skills.*
★ *Discuss different kinds of animal homes. Compare likenesses and differences.*

★ ★

Lesson Three
ONE DAY WHEN I WAS HOME . . .

Motivation

Ask the children if they have ever been lonely. Let them share the experience.

Activity

Distribute Worksheet 5. Ask for reactions to the picture.

Explain/Model

Tell the children to follow these steps when creating a story about Worksheet 5:

1. Write key words—either under the picture or on the chalkboard—that describe the picture.
2. Choose one main idea of the picture and use that idea to create a title for the story. For example: "At Home Alone."
3. Make a list of several ways to start the story—One day, Once upon a time, etc.
4. Talk about the character in the picture and how he feels.

Then have the class discuss the different ways that the story can end. Elicit a happy ending, such as a friend came to visit the boy. Draw the friend on the chair, and change the boy's sad look to a smile. Finally, have the children write the story, either together as a group or individually.

Practice

Encourage the children to draw a picture about a sad (or happy) experience they have had and to write a story about that experience.

(W)Rapping It Up

PUZZLE

Glue each child's story on heavy paper or cardboard. When the glue is dry, have the children cut their stories into puzzle-size pieces. Place each set of story pieces in an envelope for putting together and reading again at some future date.

★ ★

Extending Reading and Thinking

★ *Use the key words from the children's stories to teach language skills. For example, ask the children to find all the nouns or other parts of speech in the story. You can also ask them to choose a word from the story and substitute synonyms, or to group words from the story according to phonetic similarities.*

★ *Supply the children with a variety of art materials that they can use to construct miniature homes—perhaps even a neighborhood.*

★ ★

Name _____

NO PLACE LIKE HOME

The family needs:

to be loved

to be warm

to eat

to drink

to sleep

Name _____

A TEENY TINY BOOK

Directions: Cut out the four houses. Punch out holes in the side of each house. Put the houses in the correct order. Then make a book by tying the houses together with yarn through the holes. Listen to your teacher read the story.

1

Once upon a time there was a very sad house. The house was sad because no one lived in it.

In another town there was a very sad family. The family was sad because their home had burned to the ground in a fire.

"I am cold and scared," said the sister.

"I am hungry and thirsty," said the brother.

"I am tired," said the mother.

"We need a home," said the father.

2

One day the family packed everything they owned and got on a bus. The bus took them to the town of the sad house. Then they got off the bus and began walking. Soon it was getting dark, but the family had no place to stay for the night.

3

Then a strange thing happened. The family saw a bright light shining, and they walked toward it. The closer they came to the light the brighter it became.

The light was coming from the sad house. Soon the house began to glow. It was like daytime inside the sad house.

4

The family saw that no one was living in the house. They went inside. They felt safe and warm. They ate and drank. They snuggled close together.

"This is good," said the family. "We have a home."

And the house was not sad anymore. It was a happy home.

Name _____

THE SAD HOUSE STORY

Directions: Retell the story about The Sad House using the pictures below to help you. When you are finished, you may add these pictures to the book you made from Worksheet 1.

From *Let's Learn English: Second Language Activities for the Primary Grades*, Copyright © 1987 Scott, Foresman and Company.

Name _____

AT HOME

Directions: Write the name of the correct room on the line above each picture. Then write one of the sentences below on the line under each picture.

We are now going to eat and drink.
I am going to sleep.
I am going to wash my hands.
We are safe and warm.

Name _____

WHERE DOES IT GO?

Directions: Draw a line from each piece of furniture to the room where it goes. Then say: "The _____ goes in the _____ ."

Underline the main idea of this worksheet:

a. Kitchen and bedroom furniture
b. Putting furniture into a house
c. A stove, a table, and a TV

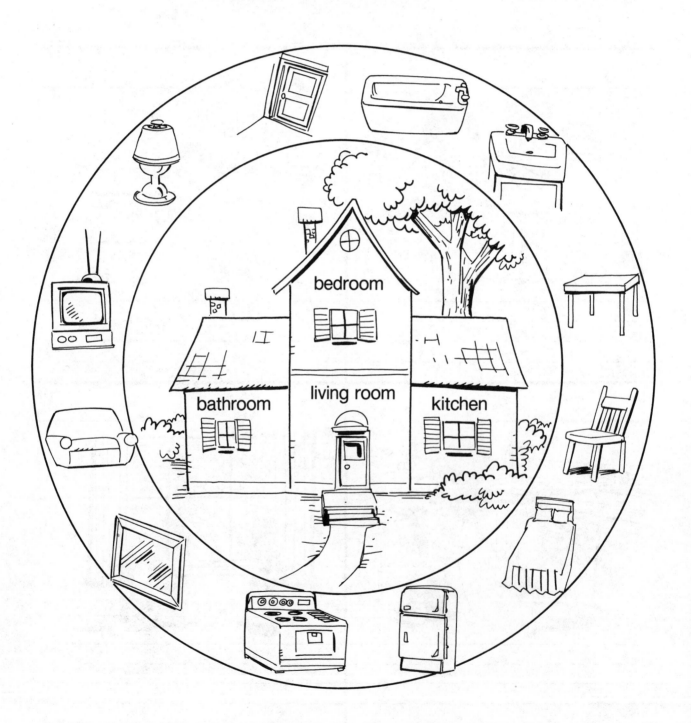

Name _____

Title: _____

Directions: Write a story about this picture. Give your story a title.

Unit Ten
SCHOOL

In this unit, children will use language as they relate to their own experiences about school. They will practice sequencing and using vocabulary relating to school.

Lesson One
THE THREE R's

Motivation

Tell the children that many school activities take place in a 1-2-3-4 order.

Activity

DISCUSSION

Discuss the three sets of pictures on the Unit Ten Theme Sheet. Point out the order of events.

Explain/Model

Give the simple example of washing hands before lunch.

1. Get soap.
2. Rub soap on hands.
3. Rinse soap off hands with water.
4. Dry hands.

Ask the children to place other school activities in sequential order.

Practice

Distribute Worksheet 1, STEPS FOR MAKING A STICK PUPPET and Worksheet 2, DOING SCHOOL WORK. Have the children practice sequencing by numbering the pictures in the correct order and completing the sentences.

(W)Rapping It Up

DRAMATICS

Have three children dramatize the following three scenes out of order:

1. Preparing to eat a sack lunch at school
2. Eating the lunch
3. Finishing lunch and going back to class

The other children decide what scene should be first, second, and last. Then have the three children act out the three scenes in the correct order.

★ ★

Extending Reading and Thinking

★ *Encourage children to create other three-scene plays and to act out their plays in either the correct or incorrect sequence. Other children must guess what each play is about and if it was done in the proper order.*

★ ★

Lesson Two
LIBRARY FUN

Motivation

Use the Theme Sheet to review correct sequence.

   From *Let's Learn English: Second Language Activities for the Primary Grades*, Copyright © 1987 Scott, Foresman and Company.

Activity

| DRAMATIZATION |

Tell the children that you will dramatize checking out a book from the school library. They are to watch and listen carefully because later you will ask them to retell what happened first, second, third, and last. Act out the following scenes:

1. Browse for a library book.
2. Select a book.
3. Check out the book.
4. Read the book.

Explain/Model

Distribute Worksheet 3, FIRST OR LAST? Help the children recall the order of events in the dramatization. Then describe a step and have the children determine if it happened first, second, third, or fourth. Finally, have the children follow the directions on the worksheet.

Practice

Distribute Worksheet 4, KITTY GETS A LIBRARY BOOK. By following the worksheet directions, children practice sequencing the story that tells what Kitty did to get a library book. When they complete the worksheet, ask the children to retell the story with the events in the correct order.

(W)Rapping It Up

| LISTING |

Ask the children to list four steps necessary for giving a book report.

★ ★

Extending Reading and Thinking

★ *Have the children list the steps—in the correct order—for making their favorite after-school snack.*

★ ★

Lesson Three
AS EASY AS ONE-TWO-THREE

Motivation

Use the Theme Sheet to review the sequence of events. Remind the children that sequence of events means that things happen in a 1-2-3-4 order.

Activity

| CHANT |

Recite the following chant:

As Easy As One-Two-Three
Everything has its order,
First, next, and last.
Come in, sit down,
Let's get to work.
As easy as one, two, three.

Everything has its order,
First, second, and third.
Come in, sit down,
Let's have some fun.
As easy as one, two, three.

Explain/Model

Explain to the children that when they read they need to be aware of certain words that help them know the order of events. Some of these words are first, next, last, then, before, after, second, third, finally, and following.

Practice

Have the children, working as a class, practice writing the steps in a process. Topics may include familiar school activities such as a painting project, eating lunch, a cut-and-paste art activity, a physical education exercise, or a game. Encourage the children to use sequence clue words when writing the steps in a process.

(W)Rapping It Up

`GAME`

Play the game "Sequence Shuffle" with the Unit Ten Theme Sheet. Have each child color and cut out all the pictures from the Theme Sheet. Each player shuffles his or her set of cards and then, on a start signal, places all of the cards in the proper sequence as quickly as possible. The winner of "Sequence Shuffle" is the first player to arrange a complete set of cards in the right order.

★ ★

Extending Reading and Thinking

★ *Give the children a textbook selection that teaches the sequencing skill. Have them underline the sequence clue words as they read.*

★ *Have the children watch as you demonstrate a simple classroom experiment such as mixing primary colors to make secondary colors. When you finish, ask the children to write the steps of the experiment in order.*

★ ★

Name _____

THE THREE R's

Reading

First

Last

Mathematics

First

Last

Writing

First

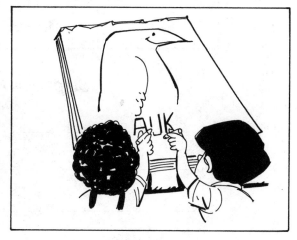

Last

Name _____

STEPS FOR MAKING A STICK PUPPET

Directions: Number the pictures below from 1 to 4 in the order they should be followed. Then fill in the blanks at the bottom of the page with the words in the boxes. When you are finished, you should have a set of directions that tells someone how to make a stick puppet.

Cut	Show	Color	Glue

Steps For Making A Stick Puppet

1. _____ the puppet.

2. _____ the puppet.

3. _____ the puppet.

4. _____ the puppet.

Name _____

DOING SCHOOL WORK

Directions: Number the pictures below from 1 to 4 in the order they should be followed. Then fill in the blanks at the bottom of the page with the words in the boxes. When you are finished, you should have a set of directions that tells someone how to do school work. Tell those steps to a friend.

Check	Do	Write	Get

Steps For Doing School Work

1. _____ paper and pencil.

2. _____ name on paper.

3. _____ the work.

4. _____ the answers.

Name _____

FIRST OR LAST?

Directions: Cut out the four pictures below. Then paste them in the correct order in the boxes.

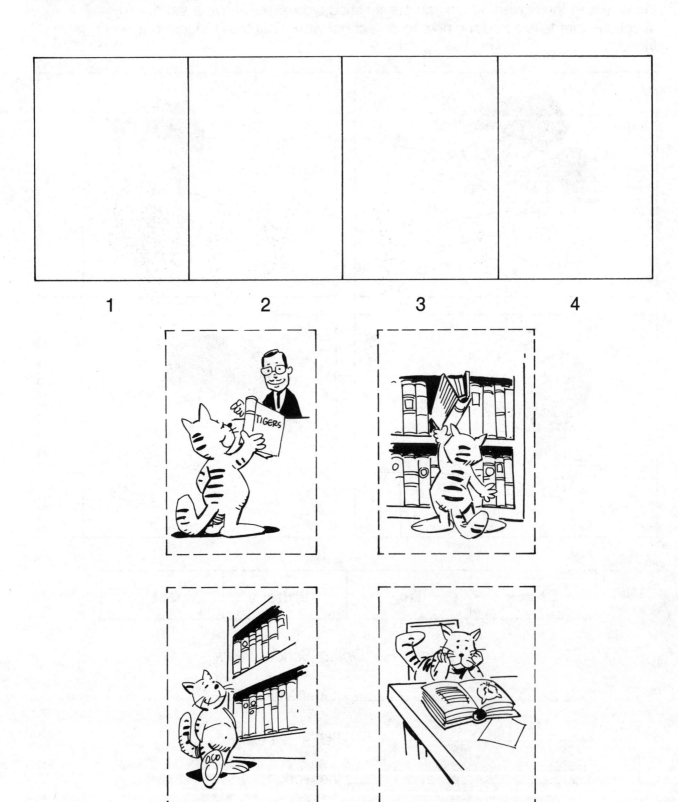

1   2   3   4

Name _____

KITTY GETS A LIBRARY BOOK

Directions: Read the story. Then fill in the blanks with the words in the boxes to tell the correct order of events.

Second	First	Last	Third

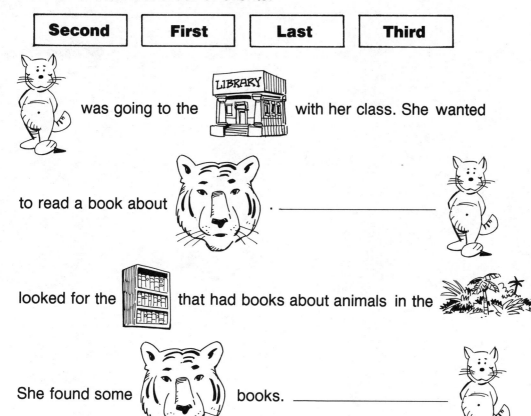

_____ was going to the [LIBRARY] with her class. She wanted

to read a book about [tiger] . _____ [kitty]

looked for the [bookshelf] that had books about animals in the [jungle] .

She found some [tiger] books. _____ [kitty]

chose the book she liked best. _____ the book was

checked out by the school [librarian] . _____ [kitty] sat

down to read the book about her cousin, the [tiger] .